Catholic Update Guide to Confession

Catholic Update
guide to
Confession

MARY CAROL KENDZIA,
Series Editor

ST. ANTHONY MESSENGER PRESS
Cincinnati, Ohio

LIBRARY OF CONGRESS CATALOGING-IN-PUBLICATION DATA

Catholic update guide to confession / Mary Carol Kendzia, series editor.

p. cm.— (Catholic update guides)

Includes bibliographical references.

ISBN 978-1-61636-003-0 (alk. paper)

1. Confession—Catholic Church. 2. Catholic Church—Doctrines. I. Kendzia, Mary Carol.

BX2265.3.C38 2011

234'.166—dc22

2011003954

Published by St. Anthony Messenger Press

28 W. Liberty St.

Cincinnati, OH 45202

www.AmericanCatholic.org

www.SAMPBooks.org

Printed in the United States of America.

Printed on acid-free paper.

11 12 13 14 15   5 4 3 2 1

Contents

About This Series

The Catholic Update guides take the best material from our best-selling newsletters and videos to bring you up-to-the-minute resources for your faith. Topically arranged for these books, the words you'll find in these pages are the same clear, concise, authoritative information you've come to expect from the nation's most trusted faith formation series. Plus, we've designed this series with a practical focus—giving the "what," "why," and "how to" for the people in the pews.

The series takes the topics most relevant to parish life—e.g., the Mass, sacraments, Scripture, the liturgical year—and draws them out in a fresh and straightforward way. The books can be read by individuals or used in a study group. They are an invaluable resource for sacramental preparation, RCIA participants, faith formation, and liturgical ministry training, and are a great tool for everyday Catholics who want to brush up on the basics.

The content for the series comes from noted authors such as Thomas Richstatter, O.F.M., Lawrence Mick, Leonard Foley, O.F.M., Carol Luebering, William H. Shannon, and others. Their theology and approach is grounded in Catholic practice and tradition, while mindful of current Church practice and teaching. We blend each author's style and approach into a voice that is clear, unified, and eminently readable.

Enrich your knowledge and practice of the Catholic faith with the helpful topics in the Catholic Update Guide series.

Mary Carol Kendzia
Series Editor

Introduction

In writing for *Catholic Update,* Thomas Richstatter, O.F.M., responds to a lot of questions Catholics have about confession, or what we more properly call "the sacrament of reconciliation." Where once there seemed to be more people waiting in line to go to confession on Saturday than there were waiting to go to Communion on Sunday, that seems to have changed. Richstatter examines the changes in the sacrament over the years and answers some of the questions he most frequently hears.

***

What happened to confession? The lines of penitents waiting to enter the confessional on Saturday afternoon seem to have disappeared. Have Catholics simply stopped going to confession? How does one celebrate the sacrament today?

When I was in grade school, each Saturday evening my mom and dad took me to church and we went to confession. I never questioned why we did this, it was simply something that good Catholics did. Now, I would explain the practice by saying that this was a way to assure that we would be in the state of sanctifying grace in order to receive holy Communion at Mass the following day, Sunday morning. Even for those of us without grave sin and who were already in the state of grace—and I certainly would place my parents in that category—Saturday confession was a way to prepare ourselves to be as holy as possible to receive the most holy sacrament of the Eucharist.

Today two things have changed: The Eucharist itself is seen as a sacrament of forgiveness; and the sacrament of reconciliation is not simply (or even primarily) a preparation for holy Communion. It has its own meaning as a wonderful sign of God's love and forgiveness.

Often I hear something like: "I'm a Catholic who still believes strongly in the value of confession but I feel unsure nowadays about the best way to celebrate this sacrament. What can I do to make confession a richer and more peaceful experience?"

If these words express your own sentiments and anxieties

about the sacrament of reconciliation, this book will give you helpful insights and even a bit of comfort.

I know, however, that there are many Catholics who, on seeing book called a "Guide to Confession," may be tempted to quip: "Why would I want a guide for doing something that I haven't done in years?!"

As someone who celebrates this sacrament from both viewpoints—that is, both as a penitent and as an officiating priest— I'm convinced that the sacrament of reconciliation is a gift for today's Church. In this book, therefore, I want to persuade Catholics of all kinds to approach this sacrament more confidently.

CHAPTER ONE

What Is Confession?

We know that confession is one of the seven sacraments. Those among us who paid attention in religion class or CCD class might remember that we're supposed to go once a year. Or is it once on Easter and once on Christmas? Or is it only if you've done something really, really bad to someone who in no way deserved it? Or maybe it's only if that nice Fr. Bob is hearing confessions this week, because he gives out the easiest penances?

But what does confession have to do with the rest of our faith lives? How does it relate to our experience of Mass? How often do we have to go? Is there such a thing as going to confession too often? Once again, Fr. Richstatter offers his wisdom on the subject.

***

The Mass and Forgiveness

When Mass was in Latin, I never really noticed how frequently the prayers spoke of the forgiveness of sins. Now, Sunday after Sunday, I (together with the whole church) hear, "May almighty God...forgive us our sins" (Penitential Rite); "You take away the sin of the world: have mercy on us" (Glory to God); "[We], though sinners, hope in your abundant mercies, graciously grant some share and fellowship with your holy Apostles and Martyrs...admit us, we beseech you, into their company, not weighing our merits, but granting us your pardon" (Eucharistic Prayer I); "Our Father... forgive us our trespasses, as we forgive those who trespass against us" (Lord's Prayer); "Behold the Lamb of God who takes away the sins of the world... Lord, I am not worthy... but only say the word and my soul shall be healed" (Invitation to Communion).

At each Eucharist we hear Christ's command: "Take this, all of you, and drink from it, for this is the chalice of my Blood, the Blood of the new and eternal covenant, which will be poured out for you and for many for the forgiveness of sins."

And in holy Communion, I am in com-union (union-with) Christ and church. As my sins distance me from Christ and the Church, holy Communion draws me back into intimate union with Christ and his members. Meals, especially ritual meals, have traditionally been times of forgiveness and reconciliation. It is not surprising, then, that for many Catholics the Sunday Eucharist has become the usual sacrament by which they experience the forgiveness of their sins.

Are Catholics Required to Go to Confession?

The current law of the church states that a person who is conscious of grave sin is not to receive the Body of the Lord (Communion) without previous sacramental confession unless there is a grave reason and there is no opportunity to confess (Canon 916).

Think, for example, of the parable of the prodigal son. The boy who had cut himself off from the life of the family was now to be readmitted to the daily family table. He admitted his fault and asked forgiveness. Yet to restore the son's place, a special celebration of reconciliation and homecoming was needed. "And get the fattened calf and kill it, and let us eat and celebrate; for this son of mine was dead and is alive again; he was lost, and is found!" (Luke 15:23–24).

For those Catholics who have cut themselves off from God and the church by serious (grave, mortal) sin and now wish to return to God's table (many Catholics find this situation rarely happens in their lives), the church offers the sacrament of reconciliation to celebrate their "homecoming." This is the only time when Catholics are *required* to celebrate the sacrament. But we celebrate reconciliation not merely because we have to, but because it is a sacrament—a sign and celebration of God showing forth his

3

mercy "by reconciling the world to himself in Christ and by making peace for all things on earth and in heaven by the blood of Christ on the cross"—as we read in the very first words of the Rite of Penance.

Confession: Serious Business

In writing about the changes in the sacrament of reconciliation that took place shortly after the Second Vatican Council, Fr. Leonard Foley, O.F.M., stresses that the bishops seemed to be prescribing the strong medicine of confession a bit more conservatively than they once had. He notes that,

> Evidently the bishops must have something deeper in mind. The most important part of knowing how to confess therefore, is the capturing of the new outlook behind the revised ritual....
>
> Leaders of the church are telling us that whether for mortal or venial sinfulness this sacrament is a very special and important celebration. It is not something to be taken lightly or routinely, or done merely to make someone "feel better" or to unload a burden of sin in an action that has no relationship with the rest of our lives. In other words, we are being asked to celebrate the sacrament seriously or, in my opinion, not at all.

Certainly there are few Catholics who can be accused of making too frequent use of the sacrament of confession, especially today, but Foley's words remind us that, in the not-so-distant past, the sacrament had become a routine for far too many. While the pendulum may have swung too far since that time, we would be wise to consider that confession—like all the sacraments of the church—is serious business and should not be abused by being taken too lightly (as was once the case) or taken too infrequently (as is more likely today).

So, how can we find a balance between avoiding confession altogether and confessing so frequently that the sacrament loses its meaning for us? A good start is to understand how this sacrament can fulfill our human needs and help us grow in our relationship with God—the subject of the next chapter.

Questions for Reflection

1. How often should you go to confession? How long has it been since your last confession?
2. How is the sacrament of reconciliation linked to the sacrament of the Eucharist?
3. When have you experienced God's forgiveness most?

CHAPTER TWO

Why Do We Go to Confession?

Apart from the laws of the church that regulate when we must go to confession, is there any benefit to receiving the sacrament? Intellectually, we know that God and the Church would not establish and insist on an empty practice, so there must be something behind it. What can confession do for us? Fr. Leonard Foley, O.F.M., explains that there is a special set of human needs addressed each time we confess our sins.

***

FIRST NEED: To "get it all out" to another human being

A long time ago the wise psalmist wrote:

> While I kept silence, my body wasted away
> through my groaning all day long.
> For day and night your hand was heavy upon me;
> my strength was dried up as by the heat of summer.
>
> Then I acknowledged my sin to you,
> and I did not hide my iniquity;
> I said "I will confess my transgressions to the Lord,"
> and you forgave the guilt of my sin.
> (Psalm 32:3–5)

Obviously, one can say that this refers to confessing to God. But it also expresses a human experience we all have had. As Archbishop Jozef Tomko of Czechoslovakia put it rather simply, "A person has an interior need to open his or her soul to another."

This is one of many cases where it is not good for man or woman to be alone. Joy and love and hope have to be shared, guilt and despair have to be shared, or they will fester into serious diseases of the spirit. We need another person to understand what we are feeling, to have compassion, "suffering-with." Then we can face up to the decision we already know we must make.

The sacrament of reconciliation isn't the only way we can do this, of course. The Bible says, "Confess your sins to one another." If you can find a better ear (and heart) than that of the priest in the confessional, you will do well to share your heart with that person, too. But we do have to unburden ourselves to *somebody*. (If you have no unburdening to do, set up a soapbox and tell everybody how you've managed that. You'll make millions.)

So, look for a wise and welcoming priest. That sounds, I realize, as though not all priests have these qualities, and unfortunately that's true. Some of us older soldiers were raised in the more formal way of celebrating the sacrament, and we may find some of the informality the new form allows (face-to-face confession, for example) a little threatening. But there are many good and holy priests who can make the experience welcoming and rewarding for you. (If this sounds too ambitious, you might want to take the advice of St. Teresa of Avila, who said she preferred a *wise* to a *holy* confessor!)

Evidently we're talking here about a confession that goes deeper than the conventional laundry list, and looks for causes rather than symptoms. My life, good or bad or both, is not a string of isolated minutes. It is a flow, with a generally consistent spirit and set of values. The friends who know me best could tell me immediately what I should talk about! As a sometime confessor, I can vouch for the relief that many people feel from the kind of confession that explores frankly one's motivations and fears, and the underlying causes of one's sinfulness. Often what is expressed is a load of *false* guilt—and that has to be "gotten out" too. And even with those who bear real guilt, the confessor is more struck with their sincerity and humility than with their sin.

Perhaps one of the most honest confessions I ever heard took place after an evening service during a parish mission. A man came into the sacristy and said, rather heartily, "Father, I'm one of those S.O.B.'s that preacher was talking about!" Then with great humility and candor he laid his life bare before me. (Big sinners usually don't take much time confessing. And often they don't need to analyze themselves to death to discover their motivations, their sinfulness.)

SECOND NEED: To "come back"

The Prodigal Son made a life decision. He chose a way of living. It took a while: Maybe he had only the glimmerings of his coming life of sin when he left home, but he let the process flow and he adopted a way of life. He had not only left his father's table literally; he had left behind what he was taught there. He was alienated, a stranger. As he later realized, he was really no longer his father's son, except in body. He had abandoned the spirit of his father's home. He was no longer in the family circle, physically and spiritually. In the agony of guilt, he felt he didn't deserve to come back that far—it would be enough to be a hired hand. But his father insisted on bringing him back to the table, equal, loved, forgiven.

One who is really guilty of a sinful life that runs so deep he or she has abandoned the table of the Lord is in the same boat as the Prodigal Son. Such persons wouldn't think of waltzing back and taking a chair with no apology. They might not even think they can ever be worthy of that table again. The purpose of the sacramental action is to be a sign of God's welcoming embrace to those persons who have strayed from home. It is a symbol (a real one, not "just" a symbol, which is meaningless) that they are being welcomed back. God indeed embraces them—and his love must be evident in the graciousness of the priest and community they return to.

It's obviously hard to think of venial sinfulness as thrusting one completely away from the table. It's more like a pouting child's pushing his chair back from the table, and a mother's saying, "Sit up and eat your carrots!"

Venial sinfulness is a way of life, too. It's the (as yet) minor selfishness that is a problem to everybody around. It's the (as yet) minor vindictiveness or thoughtlessness or stubbornness that adds one more burden to the lives of others. It's the (as yet) minor independence that frets and fumes at obedience, cooperation, docility, or the minor cowardice and apathy that can ultimately lead to spiritual death. As long as one feels this is a "minor" problem, of course, one feels no need to "get it out" or "come back."

But if it is seen as really dulling our life and chilling the spirit, a real sickness (minor, of course!), then we can be serious about it and approach the sacrament seriously. We can undertake the serious task of coming back home to our true source of life and love.

Coming back to the table—from whatever distance—implies another need:

THIRD NEED: To "believe" in sin

Many commentators have stressed the fact that we seem to have lost our sense of sin. Maybe the diminished sense of sin came about because some needed to be set free of exaggerated fears that induced a sense of guilt when there was none. On the other hand, maybe we haven't yet awakened to the real destructive power of sin oppressing the world.

It's hard to believe that anyone who has suffered the pain of war, the murder of a loved one, the loss of home or property by theft or dishonesty, the loss of a marriage by unfaithfulness or selfishness, the loss of a career or a precious relationship through alcohol or drugs or promiscuity—not to speak of the horrors of persecution, tyranny, prison—can say that "nothing is a sin anymore." For they have experienced the evil and tragedy of sin in their own bones, and in their real life experience.

History is partly—perhaps largely—the history of sin. To look at the other, more important side of the coin, history is the record of God's endless attempt to save free men and women from the abuse they repeatedly make of their freedom.

"Nothing is a sin anymore" may be the cry of those who were raised on a too-objective view of sin. Sin was too much "out there." It was a sin "out there" if you were not in the church building for Mass on Sunday. We didn't think too much about the valid reasons for staying home. (Well, yes, if you had a temperature of 109 and could throw in a broken leg, you could stay home—maybe.) People felt "guilty" nevertheless because (objective fact) they were not in church. The same was true of "feelings." We often felt compelled to confess them as sins, even though emotions of themselves have no morality and are quite useful to human life. "I had feelings of resentment, anger, etc.," we would confess—probably because some nitwit trampled our flowers, or someone in our own home treated us thoughtlessly. We weren't always told that it was God himself who gave us a whole set of powerful emotions—evidently so we would use them appropriately.

True, we were taught that there had to be "full knowledge" and "full consent of the will" for mortal sinfulness. But that "full" was not allowed to be "full." It might be argued that all that modern moral theologians have done is explore what "full" really means: full awareness, understanding, consciousness of the meaning of what I propose to do; in more common language, we'd say that, "I knew very well what I was doing."

Adding to this, then, in order for our sin to be a "real" sin, it had to be the result of a fully free decision—not one submerged in a flood of emotion, or even emotional sickness. "Full" should have meant adopting a decision that really expressed our way of life. Not that we should have been able to analyze all this and articulate it like a theologian, but it had to be there. After all, a decision that really breaks our relationship with God has to be at least as well-considered as the one whereby we buy a house, get married, or move to Idaho.

But because of the emphasis on the objective "serious matter" and an incomplete understanding of "full," there was a lot of false guilt around, as anyone who has heard confessions will testify. And this useless, distracting burden must be dumped, of course. We must throw it off if for no other reason than to be free to see and admit the real sinfulness of our lives. We cannot look at the world or into our own hearts and conclude that it is all false guilt, or that all wars and oppression are the result of someone's glandular imbalance, or that cruelty and injustice in marriage are all the result of temperamental predisposition, or that the massive deceit on which much of the world runs is caused by oedipal fixation. Somebody's causing this evil.

Of course, I can't be sure of anyone's sin but my own. But I can be sure of that. The trouble is, often I don't want to be sure. I want every explanation but the right one. We seldom admit, misquoting the cartoon character Pogo, "I have met the guilty one and it is me." It is not just "they" who sin: *I* sin.

FOURTH NEED: To see and hear forgiveness

Jesus spoke words to the adulteress: "Your sins are forgiven." He looked at people. Sometimes he embraced them. He assured the converted tax collector Zacchaeus, "Today salvation has come to your house." These people went away with Jesus' words in their ears, his image in their minds, the touch of his hands on their shoulders.

We cannot live in our minds only. It will never be enough to know theoretically that others love us, or are supposed to love us. If they do not speak to us, or look at us, we can never be sure they love us. And we can't live that way. It isn't enough to *know* that God loves us and forgives us. It's fine to "confess our sins to God" in our minds, but we have bodies. We are body-spirits, and our normal way of communicating is by bodily signs. We need to externalize or ritualize or visibly celebrate God's victory over sin. In short, we need "body language."

God obviously knows this, since he made us that way. So he sent a sign for us to look at, to listen to, to be assured by: *Jesus.* Jesus is, literally, God's "Word" to us. But I wasn't there when Jesus was visible and audible. So he left another sign—a sign of himself, his presence, his forgiveness and his love—his community. The community of Jesus—and all the small communities that make up his Church—is the living sign in the world of his power, his forgiveness, and his action.

I've long since realized the uselessness of arguing with people about what they ought to feel, think, or do. I'm convinced that people will do what is right if they experience the good involved in it. This is why we need to see, hear, and feel God's forgiveness, and that is precisely why we need sacraments—seeable-hearable-feelable-smellable-tasteable signs/symbols that give us the experience of the God who is acting through them. It is true that we need a visible community which is the sign (sacrament) of Jesus, making it possible for us to experience his love and forgiveness. Finally, this sign which is the Church is mediated through some poor human priest, who by the amazing condescension of God happens to be the obviously unworthy representative of Christ, the head of the Body called Church.

But if these three signs—sacrament, community, priest—are not a human experience, we are thrown back on that familiar old theological principle: "The sacraments work of themselves." What this means is that the most poorly conducted Mass, the coldest community, and the most mechanical priest cannot stop the grace of God. They can make it triply difficult for the poor sinner, however, whom God wants to reach not only in the depths of the heart, but in the body-spirit experience of life.

There is always a danger of a "magic" mentality where externals are concerned, as if it is merely necessary to say the right words or go through the right actions, and something happens—like putting the right coins in a Coke machine and (presto!) a cold can comes bounding down the chute. Some of this, at least, crept into the practice of the Church. That's human nature. And perhaps the falloff of confessions can be partly traced to an awareness of this.

Yet perhaps we're all yearning (but not yet quite ready) for sacramental celebrations that are deeply experienced, that really affect our lives—a "big deal" each time, not trivial, routine, or superficial. This is what the new understanding of the sacrament of confession hopes to regain. This is why the Church is trying to find ways to make the ritual celebration of the sacrament a more adequate expression of God's loving forgiveness.

FIFTH NEED: To recognize that our sin is linked with society's

The Church wrestles with the task of dealing with two subjects that are connected—but not obviously (as one man's germ–laden cough is connected with others' colds, or as one car's exhaust is part of the pollution that dims a city's light). The two subjects are "personal sin" and "structural sin" or "social sin."

The fact of sin in our world's institutions is obvious; the guilt is another matter. Because of wide-ranging modern communications, we probably know more about "man's inhumanity to man" than any other people in history: wars around the globe; the pervasiveness of terrorism; discrimination against women and minorities; the economic enslavement of large masses of people in a system that on principle is concerned with profit alone, not people; the denial of basic human needs; nations spending astronomical sums of money on unnecessary and wasteful "defense" systems; the threat of planetary death because of the overconsumption of some nations and the seemingly insurmountable poverty of others.

In using the term "structural sin," the bishops were questioning the world economic order, the workings of multinational corporations and repressive governments. In general, they used the term to refer to social, economic, and political situations and systems which produce injustices. Some of the evil in the world is just the bad decision or failing of one individual; some makes it difficult for any individual to make good moral decisions.

Reconciliation, then, is an across-the-board matter: individual, familial, social. If the human heart is not healed and converted, the transformation of unjust social structures cannot take place. On the other hand, unless unjust structures—a kind of objective sin covering the earth like pollution—are transformed, human hearts will wither or despair.

This surely adds another dimension to the question "Why do we go to confession?" We need to confess my wrongs not only to heal or save our own private soul, but to help liberate the world from its sinful patterns of operation. There is a connection between our individual sinful heart and sinful system "out there." Every time our own heart is violent or militaristic or greedy, every time we buy into a stereotype that puts down women or minorities, for example, we not only defile our own heart but contribute to or endorse the world's sinful structures.

Therefore, we not only need to confess and be healed of our private guilt but also must work for its elimination on the social level also. The sacrament of reconciliation presents us today with the task of healing and transforming our own individual hearts, as well as cooperating in Jesus' mission of healing and transforming the sinful and unfinished condition of the world.

"There are more things in heaven and earth than are thought of in your philosophy," Hamlet said to Horatio. So there are more things involved in confession than a bare recital of sins. It is reconciliation raised to the level of sacrament: the visible action of God through his community, by means of a symbolic rite that carries his own action, and that of his Body the Church. It is a moment of truth, a significant step in our never-ending conversion and that of the world. We must not mock it with triviality, or divert its thrust with false guilt. It is facing God with honesty, healthy fear and childlike confidence as sinful human beings and placing our broken lives before God's healing love, both as individuals and as members of a sinful world.

Questions for Reflection

1. What is meant by the terms "personal sin" and "structural sin"? How are these two related?

2. How are mortal and venial sins different? How can you determine whether a sin is mortal or venial?

3. Is it important to hear the words of forgiveness? Is there someone who needs to hear these words from you?

CHAPTER THREE

How Do We Go to Confession?

If you're feeling that you've been away from the sacrament of reconciliation for too long, you're not alone. Though we know the
relief and healing the sacrament can bring, a long absence from
the confessional can make the experience seem even more difficult than it really is. This chapter will reacquaint you with the
basic form of the rite, as well as give you some tips to get the most
out of your next confession.

Thomas Richstatter, O.F.M., describes the format of the sacrament of reconciliation as having four main parts. Though there
are different ways to experience the sacrament, all share this same
pattern.

***

Four Steps to Celebrating the Sacrament of Reconciliation Individually

1. Gathering. We enter the reconciliation chapel and we exchange a greeting with the priest. We can sit face-to-face with the priest or remain anonymous behind a screen. Many people worry about what the priest thinks of them when they tell him their sins. They imagine that in confessing their sins the priest sees them at their worst. Actually the very opposite is true. Everybody sins; however, only some sinners are moved to do penance. When you tell your sins to the priest and express your desire to repent, the priest sees you at your best. The priest sees you, not in your sinning, but in your repentance. As a priest I have found that many Catholics, once they have tried the face-to-face option, prefer it.

After saying hello we move to prayer. Even though there are only two people present, we are about to celebrate a sacrament of the Church, an act of worship. The whole Church is made present through the priest who is ordained to speak in the name of the Church and through the promise of Christ to be present where two or three are gathered in his name. We begin with, "In the name of the Father, and of the Son, and of the Holy Spirit." The priest will say a prayer and may invite us to pray.

2. Storytelling (Liturgy of the Word). While in this atmosphere of prayer, we turn to Scripture (perhaps the Sunday Gospel) and hear again of God's faithful love. While the reading of Scripture is optional, the Church recommends it, because it is very important for the meaning of the sacrament. It reminds us that every sacramental action is a response to the Word of God, and it provides that Word to inspire our participation in the sacrament. Although some priests will have legitimate reasons not to do so, ideally the priest will invite you to read a passage from the Bible (or he himself will read a passage).

One of the blessings of the Second Vatican Council is the increasing importance that the sacred Scriptures play in my life and in the lives of most Catholics. "When the Scriptures are read in the church, it is Christ himself who speaks" (Constitution on the Sacred Liturgy, 7). When I first started going to confession I was taught to examine my conscience in the light of the Ten Commandments. The whole moral life was divided and categorized under these ten headings. Today I form my conscience not only from the Ten Commandments, but from all of Scripture, particularly the Gospels. I find this gives a rich variety to my "confessions" as I reflect on the Scriptures in the various seasons of my life and the life of the Church.

As a child, I understood sin to be disobeying my parents or doing something that I knew they would not approve of. When I went to school, I learned that sin was breaking God's law. As an adult, I realize that sin must be understood in relation to God's love. In the Scriptures and in the experiences of our daily lives, we see how much God has loved us and continues to care for us.

When we examine our lives in the light of God's love, we come to realize that our love for God, our neighbor, and ourselves falls far short of God's love for us. When we consider the difference between these two loves—how much God has loved us and how little we have loved in return—we become aware of our sinfulness. Sin, in a sense, is basically ingratitude: our lack of response to the generosity of the loving creator. The creator calls us to life, growth, and wholeness.

Sin is the refusal of that gift of life and call to growth. To be aware of sin, we must first be aware of God's love. Those who do not see the constant role that God plays in their lives are not aware of sin. They can recognize that they do bad things or that they break the law, but sin—in this religious meaning of the word—requires a holy person or at least one who is seeking holiness. That's why reading Scripture is important for reconciliation: It helps us to understand better how God loves us. Even if your priest does not include a reading during the sacrament, you might consider reading the parable of the Prodigal Son or some other Scripture in preparation for the sacrament.

Following the reading from Scripture (or the Opening Prayer, if the Scripture is omitted) the priest invites you to say whatever is in your heart: sins, fears, joys, questions, doubts. The priest responds by applying the sacred Scripture to your situation and suggests a penance—something that you might do or a prayer you might say to show or express your conversion.

3. Reconciling. After the exchange with the priest, you turn once again to prayer. You will tell God that you are sorry for your sins—this may be a prayer that you know by heart or you may pray in your own words (a sample Act of Contrition is on page 45). Or you may find the Our Father an appropriate Act of Contrition. The priest then prays the prayer of absolution. If you are not separated by a screen, he may place his hands on your head in the biblical gesture of healing and invocation.

The words of absolution are not merely a legal formula. They are the very heart of the sacrament. While our sins disrupt and rupture the beauty and harmony of creation, God our merciful Father has restored this harmony by the paschal victory of Christ. This restoration and reconciliation give name to the sacrament: reconciliation. In the sacrament of reconciliation the Holy Spirit is sent among us "for the forgiveness of sins." The fruits of forgiveness and reconciliation are "pardon and peace." We receive these gifts of the Holy Spirit "through the ministry of the Church" and the ministry of the priest who is ordained to speak in the name of the Spirit-filled Church. The priest prays:

> God, the Father of mercies,
> through the death and resurrection of his Son
> has reconciled the world to himself
> and sent the Holy Spirit among us
> for the forgiveness of sins;

through the ministry of the Church
may God give you pardon and peace,
and I absolve you from your sins
in the name of the Father, and of the Son,
and of the Holy Spirit.

You answer: "Amen."

When we confess our sinfulness in the sacrament of reconciliation, our word of sorrow meets God's word of forgiveness and that meeting blossoms into *shalom*, wholeness, peace. This is why we can speak of "celebrating" the sacrament of reconciliation. We celebrate God's gift of peace.

4. Commissioning. The individual rite closes very simply. The priest says: "The Lord has freed you from your sins. Go in peace;" or: "Go in peace and God bless you" or some similar words of dismissal. You respond: "Amen," or "Thank you, Father."

When you compare this way of celebrating the sacrament with the way the Catholics "went to confession" decades ago, not much seems to have changed, at least externally. We do now basically what we did then. But the primary focus of the rite has changed. As in all acts of worship, the focus of the sacrament of reconciliation is on God and what God does. The focus of confession was often on me and my sinfulness. Even in naming the sacrament we have moved from "confession" (what we do) to "reconciliation" (what God does).

Celebrating the Sacrament of Reconciliation Communally

One of the "new" ways we celebration the sacrament of reconciliation is as a community. Some parishes have embraced this new form enthusiastically, while others offer it only occasionally, as though it were a poor substitute for "real" confession. The overall movement of the sacrament is the same as for individual confession, but here is an outline to help you feel more comfortable in a communal setting.

Gathering Rites

As the community begins coming together, sometimes a minister of hospitality at the door of the church will say hello and give out a participation aid listing the hymns, the prayers to be said aloud, and any directions for participating actively in the sacrament. You might also find some of this information in the back of the church before the celebration begins. To help bring the assembly together, a typical gathering rite might consist of a hymn, a liturgical hello, and a prayer by the priest leading the celebration.

Celebrating the Word of God

At this time we hear of God's love for us, God's mercy and forgiveness. This part of the rite will probably remind you of Sunday Mass with Scripture readings and a homily.

Our Response to the Word of God

Having heard how much God loves us, we examine how we have loved God and our neighbor in return. There will be an examination of conscience in the light of the Scriptures, an act of contrition, and a procession to the confessors for individual confession and absolution.

Communal Celebration of the Rite of Reconciliation

Now we celebrate God's gift of reconciliation. This part of the celebration might typically include a proclamation of praise and thanksgiving for God's mercy, the Lord's Prayer, the Sign of Peace, a song of thanksgiving, and a Concluding Prayer.

Commissioning Rites

A blessing and dismissal are given, sending us forth with gratitude to carry God's peace into the world.

Ten Tips to a Better Confession

Whether you plan to celebrate the sacrament individually or with your parish community, these tips can help you better prepare for confession.

1. Focus on what's most important. I have found that many Catholics have less than pleasant experiences with the sacrament of reconciliation because they miss the real point of the sacrament. I think the "real point" can be found in the story I one heard from a saintly and learned German pastor, Fr. Bernard Häring:

> One Sunday afternoon in the 1930s in a little parish in Germany where he was pastor, Fr. Häring was leading the customary Sunday afternoon parish Vesper service with religious instruction and Benediction. This particular Sunday he was talking about confession.
>
> "What is the most important thing about confession?" he asked. A woman in the front pew responded: "Telling your sins to the priest. That's why we call it confession." Fr. Häring said, "Confessing the sins is important, but it's not the most important thing." A man towards the back called out: "Contrition! Being sorry for your sins! The whole thing doesn't work without contrition." Fr. Häring said, "True, it doesn't 'work' without contrition; but I don't think contrition is the most important thing." A man over on St. Joseph's side spoke up: "It's the examination of conscience. Unless you examine your conscience, you don't know what you have to be sorry for and what to confess." Fr. Häring still wasn't satisfied.
>
> An uneasy silence fell over the church. Then a little girl in the second pew said: "Father, I know what is most important. It's what Jesus does!"

It's what Jesus does! That's the most important thing, the thing we should focus upon. The examination of conscience, sorrow for sin, telling the sins to the priest—these are all important. But you will have a more positive experience of the sacrament if your focus is on what Jesus does.

In the sacrament of reconciliation Jesus announces to us, through the Church and its ministers, that our sins are forgiven and that we are loved by God. We hear the voice of Christ: "Go in peace, your sins are forgiven." This is what Jesus does. This is his gift of reconciliation.

2. Name it "Reconciliation." Names are important. The sacrament of reconciliation has had several different names. In the recent past, bishops, theologians, and Church documents have consistently called this sacrament the "sacrament of penance" and called those going to the sacrament "penitents." This language has never been popular with the Catholic laity who used the names "confession," "confessor" and "confessional." Your experience of the sacrament will be enriched if you name the sacrament—and think about it as—"reconciliation." "Confession" only names one part of the sacrament, and not the most important part at that. Reconciliation names what is most important, what Jesus does. "Sacrament of reconciliation" is the name used in the rite itself and was the name preferred by Pope Paul VI who issued the new ritual.

The word *reconciliation* is rich in meaning. It suggests the gift of God's forgiveness and the removal of the barriers we place between ourselves, our community and our God. Reconciliation means the rebridging of the gap between God and us and between ourselves and others. It also suggests the deep peace that comes from being brought back into harmony with God, with sisters and brothers and with the whole of creation.

3. See the advantages of communal celebration. The revised rite of the sacrament of reconciliation was given to the Church by Pope Paul VI on December 2, 1973. The new rite presents the sacrament in three different ritual forms, three different shapes: (1) Rite for Reconciliation of Individual Penitents; (2) Rite for Reconciliation of Several Penitents with Individual Confession and Absolution; (3) Rite for Reconciliation of Several Penitents with General Confession and Absolution.

The first form—The Rite for Reconciliation of Individual Penitents—is similar to the way most Roman Catholics remember "confession." It is the form we discussed on page 22.

The second form—The Rite of Reconciliation of Several Penitents with Individual Confession and Absolution—is described on page 27.

The third form—The Rite for Reconciliation of Several Penitents with General Confession and Absolution—is similar to the preceding form except that the penitent need not mention each serious sin individually and the prayer of absolution is given collectively or "generally" to all those gathered to celebrate the sacrament (general absolution). This rite (the third form) with general absolution is not widely used in the United States.

While "Tip Three" (recommending a communal celebration) might refer to either form two or three, it is the second form— The Rite for Reconciliation of Several Penitents with Individual Confession and Absolution—which, I believe, deserves the greatest attention here, especially for those who find that the practice of individual "confession" as we knew it in the past does not fit their needs.

For some Catholics the very idea of a communal celebration of the sacrament may seem strange, for there are very few things that we would consider more personal and private than our sins and our sinfulness. But this is only partly true. Our sins are personal but they are never private. Pope John Paul II clearly affirmed that "there is no sin, not even the most intimate and secret one, the most strictly individual one, that exclusively concerns the person committing it.... Every sin has repercussions on the entire ecclesial body and the whole human family" (Reconciliation and Penance, 16). As sin affects the community so reconciliation affects the community. And a communal celebration of the sacrament says this most clearly.

As our sin is both personal and communal, a celebration of reconciliation which is both personal and communal will, in many cases, be the form of the sacrament which will be most helpful. The Second Vatican Council instructs us that "whenever rites...make provision for communal celebration involving the presence and active participation of the faithful,...this way of celebrating them is to be preferred, as far as possible, to a celebration that is individual and, so to speak, private" (Constitution on the Sacred Liturgy, 27).

The Holy Father Pope Paul VI, after promulgating the revision of the sacrament of reconciliation, said to a general audience on April 3, 1974, that he hoped this communal rite, that is, the second form, would "become the normal way of celebration." And indeed this is the rite which is becoming more and more popular in Catholic parishes.

4. Know what you want. There are many reasons why you might want to talk to a priest: You might want advice, counseling, moral guidance, help with your marriage, spiritual direction, or you might just want to talk to someone. It is important to know what you want. While you might want counseling or help with your marriage at a certain time in your life, for example, none of these really requires a priest-and a priest may not be the best person to meet these needs for you. More importantly, none of these things is the principal focus of the sacrament of reconciliation. The sacrament is the proclamation of reconciliation with God and with the Church. If that is what you want, choose the sacrament, but it's important to know what you want.

It is the growing conviction of many priests and liturgists that the other reasons for "talking to a priest" mentioned above (counseling, spiritual direction and so on) are separate and distinct things. And they often work best outside the sacrament.

A good silver table knife doesn't work as well as a screwdriver. But when a screw comes loose on the refrigerator door and the knives are right there while the screwdriver hasn't been seen since last Christmas, we often reach for the handiest thing. Sometimes it will get the job done, but it isn't good for the knife. Many Catholics have become dissatisfied with "confession" because they wanted it to do something it was not intended to do.

5. Don't use the sacrament as a substitute. The sacrament of reconciliation works best when you have already achieved some degree of reconciliation before celebrating the sacrament. Confessing "I am an alcoholic" is no substitute for going to Alcoholics Anonymous. To confess, "My spouse and I have started to yell and hit one another," is no substitute for seeking marriage counseling. Telling your confessor, "I get so angry when the neighbor's children play outside my bedroom window when I am trying to sleep," is no substitute for speaking to your neighbor and explaining your needs.

6. Talk about sin—not just "guilt." Many of us first received our "technical" knowledge about sin when we were children being prepared for our First Confession. We often learned that sin was "not keeping the rules" set down by the adults. For example we might confess, "I disobeyed my mommy and daddy three times." As we grow and mature our internal "list of rules" (what some call the "superego") grows also and we gather more and more "shoulds" and "oughts." Whenever we break one of these rules, intentionally or not, we feel guilty. Guilt is not the same as sin.

Sin, in a Christian perspective, is not merely "breaking the rules." For the mature Christian, sin is understood in relation to love. God has loved us so much, and we have so often failed to return that love. When we examine our lives in the light of the message of Jesus we find that Jesus calls us to wholeness, to maturity; he came that we might have life and have it abundantly. For an adult Christian, sin is more than just breaking the rules; sin is the failure to grow. Sin is being today like you were yesterday. Sin is the failure to respond to the love God has shown us in Christ Jesus. This is why the proclamation of the Word of God now has such a prominent place in the sacrament of reconciliation. It is the Word of God which convicts us of sin and which invites us to conversion.

One of the "strange" things about the Christian understanding of sin is that Christians become more aware of sin in proportion to their growth in holiness. The more we love, the more we know how much the lover is offended. The great saints really knew about sin. St. Francis of Assisi, as he lay dying, claimed he was the greatest of sinners. At one time I thought this was just the pious rambling of an unearthly man; but now I see that this was the honest realization of a great lover. My experience has often been that people's desire for the Sacrament of Reconciliation is in proportion to their holiness, not their sinfulness.

7. Examine your life in the light of the word of God. Formerly we came to church for confession knowing ahead of time what our sins were and what we were going to say. This might not always be such a good idea. It's important to come with an open mind. Don't decide finally on your sins until you participate in the celebration. Let the readings and the liturgical season, and the rite itself, help you to come to see what your sins are. During Advent, confess Advent sins (for example, how have I blocked the coming of God's reign?); during Lent confess Lent sins (for example, how have I failed to live my baptismal promises?).

During proclamation of the Scriptures, concentrate on God's love for you. The laws can give us a list of what we did wrong but the laws have no power to help us convert. The love of God has that power. As we hear the proclamation of God's love for us, we are confronted with our own response to that love. Does our love measure up to that of Jesus who said: "This is my commandment, that you love one another as I have loved you" (John 15:12)? It is our common experience that we have fallen short; we have not loved enough.

The Ten Commandments are but one small part of the Bible. Some Catholics have found that restricting their examination to the Ten Commandments led them to routine confessions, boredom and eventually dissatisfaction with the sacrament of reconciliation. The whole of sacred Scripture is for our instruction.

For example, if you are meditating on the story in John's Gospel about the cure of the man born blind, you might confess: "Father, I am sorry for the times I have been blinded by my desire to win the approval of others." Or: "I am sorry for the times I blame others for my problems." Or: "I wish to confess the times I have not seen the need to rest and go slow."

If these methods of examing your conscience don't work for you, try the model based on the three theological virtues (faith, hope, and love) found in the Appendix.

8. Pick the right time. My experience has been that people celebrate the sacrament most fruitfully when the celebration is occasioned by some important event in their lives. This event might be the yearly recurring cycle of the great solemnities of Easter and Christmas. It might be a milestone or turning point in their life's journey, for example, preparing for marriage or at the time of a spiritual retreat. Families often celebrate reconciliation together when one of their children celebrates the sacrament for the first time. Lent has always been an especially appropriate time for the sacrament of reconciliation.

If you prefer to celebrate the sacrament with the communal rite, The Rite for Reconciliation of Several Penitents with Individual Confession and Absolution, you are most likely to find it offered in your parish during Lent and Advent, and at the time when families celebrate first reconciliation with their children.

9. Experience reconciliation in a variety of ways. The reconciliation found in the sacrament is improved when you experience reconciliation in various ways. Catholics report that the most common ways in which they experience reconciliation apart from the sacrament of reconciliation are: by receiving the Eucharist (84 percent), by personal prayer (78 percent), by making an Act of Contrition (64 percent), by talking with a friend (52 percent), by helping someone in need (45 percent) and by reading the Bible (45 percent) (*Reflections on the Sacrament of Penance in Catholic Life Today*).

10. Be open to receiving a gift. "Peace be with you. As the Father has sent me, so I send you" (John 20:21). Peace is the Easter gift of the Risen Lord. Christ commissioned his followers to continue his mission of healing, forgiveness, and reconciliation-his mission of bringing peace. Peace is the "gift" of the sacrament of reconciliation. This is why we can speak of celebrating the sacrament of reconciliation.

There is joy in heaven when a sinner repents. What is loosed on earth is loosed in heaven and what is celebrated heaven is celebrated on earth. My parish holds a celebration with cookies and punch for the children and their families following their first celebration of the sacrament. How things have changed! I never thought of a party when I made my first confession. But then, my focus was on what I had done and not on what Jesus does.

For several years when I first started my ministry of reconciliation as a priest I worried about when I could "give absolution" and when I had to refuse it. Slowly I began to realize that the real problem is not the giving absolution but in helping people hear it. Too few people really hear what Jesus is doing for them. Too few people actually hear and experience, "Go in peace, your sins are forgiven." But those who do hear (and the new way of celebrating the sacrament helps us to hear these words of peace much more clearly than our former rite) receive a gift. And they know they have received a gift.

Why do I "go to confession?" To receive the gift of reconciliation. The gift is offered to you also. It's there for the asking.

Conclusion

Though it is not quite the habit it once was, the sacrament of reconciliation is still a vital part of the Church's ministry. If you are new to the Church or have been away from the sacrament for a while, we hope that the information in this book will help you understand confession better and inspire you to make it part of your practice of the faith. Remember that confession can be a requirement of the faith (as we discussed in chapter one), but that it exists for our benefit, not our burden.

If you still have questions or concerns, check out some of the other resources on this topic from *Catholic Update* by visiting our website (www.AmericanCatholic.org). Or, just call your parish priest. He'll be only too happy to welcome you to this sacrament of grace.

Appendix

An Examination of Conscience

Many of us are familiar with preparing for confession by going through the Ten Commandments to see where we've fallen short of the mark. Another practice to consider is recommended by Fr. John Hardon, S.J., who suggests that we ask ourselves how well we're living the three theological virtues—faith, hope, and love.

Faith

Do I make an honest effort to grow in the virtue of faith
every day?

Do I pray daily for an increase of faith?

What have I done today to externally profess my faith?

Do I make a serious effort to resolve difficulties that may
arise about my faith?

Do I ever defend my faith, prudently and charitably,
when someone says something contrary to what I
know is to be believed?

Have I helped someone overcome a difficulty against the faith?

Hope

Do I immediately say a short prayer when I find myself getting discouraged?

Do I dwell on my worries instead of dismissing them from my mind?

Do I fail in the virtue of hope by my attachment to the things of this world?

Do I try to see God's providence in everything that happens in my life?

Do I try to see everything from the viewpoint of eternity?

How often today have I complained, even internally?

Love

Have I told God today that I love him?

Have I failed in charity by speaking unkindly about others?

Is there someone that I consciously avoid because I dislike the person?

Am I given to dwelling on other people's weaknesses or faults?

Have I been cheerful today in my dealings with others?

Do I control my uncharitable thoughts as soon as they arise in my mind?

Did I pray for others today?

Have I controlled my emotions when someone irritated me?

Have I performed any sacrifice today for someone?

An Act of Contrition

This is a traditional Act of Contrition, which many of us memorized in grade school. It is offered here to refresh your memory or help you think of your own Act of Contrition.

O my God, I am heartily sorry for having offended Thee, and I detest all my sins, because I dread the loss of heaven, and the pains of hell; but most of all because they offend Thee, my God, Who are all good and deserving of all my love. I firmly resolve, with the help of Thy grace, to confess my sins, to do penance, and to amend my life.

Amen.

Sources

Some of the information in this book originally appeared in:

Richstatter, Thomas, O.F.M. "Ten Tips for Better Confessions," *Catholic Update,* August 1990.

_____. "How to Celebrate the Sacrament of Reconciliation Today," *Catholic Update,* August 2000.

Foley, Leonard, O.F.M., How to Go to Confession Using the New Ritual," *Catholic Update,* January 1976.

_____. "Why Confess My Sins?" *Catholic Update,* March 1984.

The God Who Reconciles. Catholic Update video.

The Church Celebrates the Reconciling God. Catholic Update video.

Contributors

Leonard Foley, O.F.M., is the author of many *Catholic Update*s and the bestselling books *Believing in Jesus: A Popular Overview of the Catholic Faith* and *Saint of the Day: Lives, Lessons, and Feasts.*

Thomas Richstatter, O.F.M., has a doctorate in liturgy and sacramental theology from the Institut Catholique of Paris. A popular writer and lecturer, Father Richstatter teaches courses on the sacraments at St. Meinrad (Indiana) School of Theology.